Programming

For Beginners

Quick Start Guide

Ray Yao

About the Authors: Ray Yao's Team

Certified PHP engineer by Zend, USA

Certified JAVA programmer by Sun, USA

Certified SCWCD developer by Oracle, USA

Certified A+ professional by CompTIA, USA

Certified ASP. NET expert by Microsoft, USA

Certified MCP professional by Microsoft, USA

Certified TECHNOLOGY specialist by Microsoft, USA

Certified NETWORK+ professional by CompTIA, USA

www.amazon.com/author/ray-yao

About This Book

"R Programming" is a textbook for high school and college students; it covers all essential R language knowledge. You can learn complete primary skills of R programming fast and easily.

The textbook includes a lot of practical examples for beginners and includes exercises for the college final exam, the engineer certification exam, and the job interview exam.

"R Programming" is a useful textbook for beginners. The straightforward definitions, the plain examples, the elaborate explanations and the neat layout feature this helpful and educative book. You will be impressed by its distinctive and tidy writing style. Reading this book is a great enjoyment!

Note

This book is only suitable for R programming beginners, high school students and college students; it is not for the experienced R programmers.

Kindle Books by Ray Yao

C# Cheat Sheet

C++ Cheat Sheet

JAVA Cheat Sheet

JavaScript Cheat Sheet

PHP MySQL Cheat Sheet

Python Cheat Sheet

Html Css Cheat Sheet

Linux Command Line

Paperback Books by Ray Yao

C# Cheat Sheet

C++ Cheat Sheet

JAVA Cheat Sheet

JavaScript Cheat Sheet

PHP MySQL Cheat Sheet

Python Cheat Sheet

Html Css Cheat Sheet

Linux Command Line

(Each Cheat Sheet contains more than 300 examples, more than 300 outputs, and more than 300 explanations.)

Table of Contents

Chapter 8 163

Appendix   Q & A 181

Recommended Books by Ray Yao........198

Chapter 1

R Introduction

What is R language?

R is the language and operating environment for statistic, analysis and drawing. R is free, open source software for the GNU system. It is an excellent tool for statistical calculating and statistical drawing.

R language was created by Ross Ihaka and Robert Gentleman at the University of Auckland in New Zealand. The application of R language in reality mainly includes the following:

1. Data science

2. Statistical calculation

3. Machine learning

R language developmental history

The R language was originally designed and developed by Ross Ihaka and Robert Gentleman in New Zealand. It was first released to the public in 1993. Many people contributed to R by contributing code and error reports. Since mid-1997, several core groups have been able to modify the R source code.

Feature of R language

R is a complete set of data processing calculation and mapping software system, whose functions include: data storage and processing system, array operation tool, complete and coherent statistical analysis tools, excellent statistical drawing function;

R is a simple and powerful programming language that can manipulate data input and output, branch loops, and user customizable functions.

R is not only statistical software as a mathematical environment, but also provides a number of statistical tools for users to specify a database and parameters to conduct a statistical analysis and then get the perfect results.

The most excellent feature of R language is that it can provide a lot of integrated statistical tools, various mathematical and statistical calculation functions, so that users can flexibly carry out data analysis and even create statistical calculation methods that meet their needs.

R Installation

Please download:

R 3.5.1 for Windows (62 megabytes, 32/64 bit).

https://cran.r-project.org/bin/windows/base/

1. Download the R installer.

2. Double click the R installer, install the R to computer.

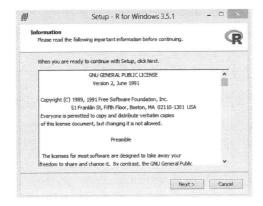

3. Click Next, install R to default folder.

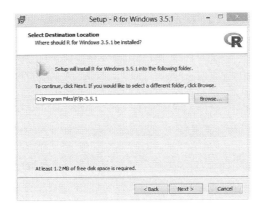

4. Click Next, Select all items.

5. Click Next, Select "Accept Default".

6. Click Next, create the program shortcut.

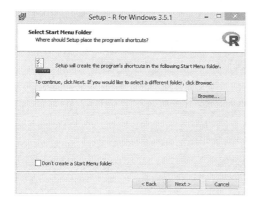

7. Click Next, select additional shortcuts.

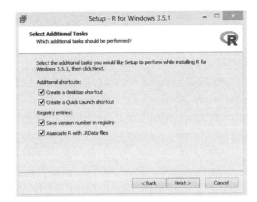

8. Click Next, complete the installation.

RGui

RGui is used to run the R program.

The R icon on the desktop is:

R x64 3.5.1

In RGui, there are two ways to run the R program:

1. R Console. 2. R Editor

R Console

R Console is used to run commands one by one; it can interact with the user.

Please **double click R icon** on the desktop, we can immediately open the R Console like this:

```
R R Console

R version 4.2.0 (2022-04-22 ucrt) -- "Vigorous Calisthenics"
Copyright (C) 2022 The R Foundation for Statistical Computing
Platform: x86_64-w64-mingw32/x64 (64-bit)

R is free software and comes with ABSOLUTELY NO WARRANTY.
You are welcome to redistribute it under certain conditions.
Type 'license()' or 'licence()' for distribution details.

  Natural language support but running in an English locale

R is a collaborative project with many contributors.
Type 'contributors()' for more information and
'citation()' on how to cite R or R packages in publications.

Type 'demo()' for some demos, 'help()' for on-line help, or
'help.start()' for an HTML browser interface to help.
Type 'q()' to quit R.

> |
```

We can see a red ">" prompt, which means that we are in the R Console now. We can input R commands beside the ">" prompt.

R Editor

R Editor is used to run the whole R program at one time instead of running R command one by one.

Click "**File**" > "**New Script**" > "**Windows**" > "**Tile Vertically**", we can open the R Editor like this:

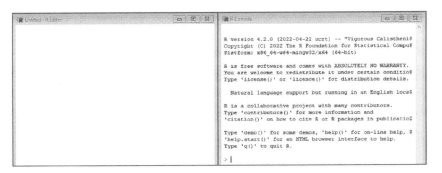

The left side is R Editor. The right side is R Console.

R Editor is empty now, which means that we can input the whole R program into the editor. When the whole R program is ready, we can click "**Edit**", and "**Run All**" to run the program, the result will appear in the R console.

Run Code in R Console

Please open the R Console, input the following R commands to it, press "Enter" key after inputting every command.

Example 1.1

```
> myText <- "Hello, World!"

> print(myText)
```

Output:

[1] Hello, World!

Explanation:

">" is an R input prompt.

"myText" is a variable. "Hello, World!" is a value.

"<-" is an assignment symbol.

"print(myText)" outputs the value of myText.

In the output:

[1] means that the first element number in the current line is 1, because R language is vectorized, any value is considered to be a vector. We will further study vector later. For example:

[10] means that the first element number in the current line is 10.

Run Code in R Editor

Please open the RGui, click "**File**" > "**New Script**" > "**Windows**" > "**Tile Vertically**" to open the R editor, input the codes as follows:

Example 1.2

```
myText <- "Hi, My Friends!"

print ( myText )
```

Please click "**Edit**" > "**Run All**" to run the program, then you can see the output in the **R Console** window.

Output:

[1] Hi, My Friends!

Explanation:

 "myText" is a variable. "Hi, My Friends!" is a value.

"<-" is an assignment operator.

"print(myText)" outputs the value of myText. In the output:

[1] means that the first element number in the current line is 1.

The output result always appears in the R console.

Comment

Comments are used to explain the code, and make the code easier understandable. Comments are ignored by the interpreter while the program is executed.

```
#
```

is a comment symbol.

Example 1.3

```
myText <- "Hello, World!"    # "myText" is a variable.
print ( myText)    # outputs the value of myText.
```

Output:

[1] Hello, World!

Explanation:

"myText" is a variable. is an R comment.

outputs the value of myText. is an R comment too.

Simple Example

Example:

```
10 + 20
name <- "Smith"
name    # show the value of name
age <- 28
age     # show the value of age
```

Output:

```
> 10 + 20
[1] 30
> name <- "Smith"
> name    # show the value of name
[1] "Smith"
> age <- 28
> age     # show the value of age
[1] 28
>
```

Explanation:

"name" and "age" are two variables, "Smith" and "28" are two values.

[1] indicates the output result.

Summary

R is the language and operating environment for statistic, analysis and drawing. R is free, open source software for the GNU system. It is an excellent tool for statistical calculating and statistical drawing.

">" is an R input prompt.

"<-" is an assignment operator.

"print(myText)" outputs the value of myText.

In the output:

[1] means that the first element number in the current line is 1.

[10] means that the first element number in the current line is 10.

RGui includes an R Editor and an R Console.

"#" a symbol that is used in R comment.

Chapter 2

Data Type

Data type: the type of an element value in a variable mainly includes: numeric, character, logical, integer, complex type.

The syntax to check the data type of a variable is:

```
class(variable)
```

"class(variable)" can check the data type of a variable.

1. Numeric type: the value is a real number.

> v <- 100

> **class(v)**

[1] "numeric"   # data type is numeric

2. Character type: the value is a string.

> v <- "100"

> **class (v)**

[1] "character"   # data type is character.

3. Logical type: the value is false or true.

```
> v <- F      # F is false,  T is true.
> class (v)
[1] "logical"    # data type is logical.
```

4. Integer type: the value is an integer.

```
> v <-  100L
> class(v)
[1] "integer"    # data type is integer.
```

5. Complex type: the value is a complex number.

```
> v <- 6+8i
> class(v)
[1] "complex"   # data type is complex.
```

Variables

Variable is the temporary storage place of the data. The value of a variable can change at any time during the operation of the program. Variables can be accessed through variable names.

A valid variable name should consist of a letter, a number, an underscore or a dot.

A variable name cannot begin with a number or underscore.

A variable can start with a dot, but it cannot be followed by a number.

For example:

Variable Name	Validity
myVariable	valid
myVariable%	invalid
my_Variable	valid
_myVariable	invalid
myVariable28	valid
26myVariable	invalid
.myVariable	valid
.123	invalid

Variable Assignment

---

variable <- value

variable = value

value -> variable   # note: -> is a rightward assignment

For example:

> x <- 100   # assign the value 100 to the variable x

> y <- 200 + 300   # assign the value 500 to the variable y

> z <- x+y   # assign the value x & y to variable z

or

> x = 100   # assign the value 100 to the variable x

> y = 200 + 300   # assign the value 500 to the variable y

> z = x+y   # assign the value x & y to variable z

or

> 100 -> x   # assign the value 100 to the variable x

> 200 + 300 -> y   # assign the value 500 to the variable y

> x + y -> z   # assign the value x & y to variable z

C( ) function

In R language, an object that has both magnitude and direction is called a vector. The syntax to create a vector is:

```
c( "element1", "element2", "element3", ...)
```

When we want to create a vector with multiple elements, we should use the c( ) function, which means to combine elements into a vector.

Example 2.1

```
# create a vector.
colors <- c("blue","pink","gray")
print(colors)
```

Output:

[1] "blue" "pink" "gray"

Explanation:

"colors <- c("blue","pink","gray")" creates a vector "colors".

c(...) is used to create a vector.

Vector Assignment

The following is the examples of vector assignment.

Example 2.2

```
# Assignment using a leftward operator.

var01 <- c(0,1,2)

print(var01)
```

[1] 0 1 2

```
# Assignment using an equal operator.

var02 = c(3,4,5)

print(var02)
```

[1] 3 4 5

```
# Assignment using a rightward operator.

c(6,7,8) -> var03

print(var03)
```

[1] 6 7 8

Print Value of Variable

cat (variable)

cat() function can output the contents to the screen.

cat() function can output the contents to a file.

cat() function can output the contents continuously.

Example 2.3

```
> # Assignment using a leftward operator.
> var01 <-  c(0,1,2)
> cat(var01)
0 1 2>    # output 0 1 2

>

>

> # Assignment using an equal operator.
> var02 = c(3,4,5)
> cat(var02)
3 4 5>    # output 3 4 5
```

```
>

> # Assignment using a rightward operator.

> c(6,7,8) -> var03

> cat(var03)

6 7 8>    # output 6 7 8

>

>

> # Using print() statement.

> c(6,7,8) -> var03

> print(var03)

[1] 6 7 8    # output 6 7 8
```

Search Variables

The syntax to list the working variable is:

```
ls( )
```

ls() can find out the current working variables.

(we need to restart RGui before running the following program)

Example 2.4

```
x<- 100

y = 200

300 -> z

ls()
```

Output:

[1] "x"   "y"   "z"

Explanation:

ls() finds out the current working variables "x", "y", "z".

Match Variables

ls(pattern = "variableName")

"ls(pattern = "variableName")" lists the variables that match the pattern with the variableName.

Example 2.5

```
var1<- 100

var2<- 200

var3<- 300

ls(pattern="var")
```

Output:

[1] "var1" "var2" "var3"

Explanation:

ls(pattern="var") lists the variables containing the name "var".

Remove Variables

```
rm( variableName)
```

rm(variableName) can remove the specified variable. After a variable has been removed, the output will show the error message.

Example 2.6

```
rm(var3)
print(var3)
```

Output:

Error in print(var3) : object 'var3' not found.

Explanation:

rm(var3) removes the specified variable "var3".

Summary

is a comment symbol.

"class(variable)" can check the data type of a variable.

A valid variable name should consist of a letter, a number, an underscore or a dot.

Three ways of Variable Assignment:

variable <- value

variable = value

value -> variable

When you want to create a vector with multiple elements, you should use the c( ) function, which means to combine elements into a vector.

The cat( ) function can output the value of a variable to the screen as well as to a file, and can print the output continuously.

ls() can find out the current working variables.

"ls(pattern = "variableName")" lists the variables that match the pattern with the variableName.

rm(variableName) can remove the specified variable. After a variable has been removed, the output will show the error message.

Chapter 3

Operators

An operator is a symbol that tells the compiler to perform a specific mathematical or logical operation.

R Language provides operators of the following types:

Arithmetic operator (+, -, *, /)

Relational operator (>, <, ==, !=, <=, >=)

Logical operator (&, ||, !)

Assignment operator (<-, <<-, ->, ->>)

Other operators (: , %in%)

Addition

```
+
```

One vector adds another.

Example 3.1

```
a1 <- c(1, 4, 7)

a2 <- c(2, 5, 8)

print(a1 + a2)
```

Output:

[1] 3 9 15

Explanation:

(a1 + a2): Vector a1 adds vector a2.

Subtraction

```
-
```

One vector subtracts another.

Example 3.2

```
s1<- c(3, 6, 9)
s2<- c(5, 3, 8)
print(s1 - s2)
```

Output:

[1] -2 3 1

Explanation:

(s1 - s2): Vector s1 subtracts vector s2.

Multiplication

```
*
```

One vector multiplies another.

Example 3.3

```
m1<- c(2, 5, 8)
m2<- c(3, 6, 9)
print(m1*m2)
```

Output:

[1] 6 30 72

Explanation:

(m1*m2): One vector m1 multiplies another m2.

Division

```
/
```

The first vector divided by the second vector

Example 3.4

```
d1 <- c(6,8,9)
d2 <- c(2,4,3)
print(d1 / d2)
```

Output:

[1] 3 2 3

Explanation:

(d1/d2): Vector d1 divided by the vector d2.

Remainder

%%

The first vector is divided by the second vector, then gets the remainder.

Example 3.5

```
r1<- c(10,13,19)

r2<- c(3,4,5)

print(r1%%r2)
```

Output:

[1] 1 1 4

Explanation:

(r1%%r2): The first vector r1 divided by the second vector r2, then gets the remainder 1,1,4.

Modulus

```
% / %
```

The first vector divided by the second vector, and then gets the modulus.

Example 3.6

```
r1<- c(10,13,19)
r2<- c(3,4,5)
print(r1 %/% r2)
```

Output:

[1] 3 3 3

Explanation:

(r1%/%r2): The first vector r1 divided by the second vector r2, and then gets the modulus 3,3,3.

Exponentiation

```
^
```

The first vector is raised to the exponent of the second vector.

Example 3.7

```
e1<- c(2,3,4)

e2<- c(3,2,2)

print(e1^e2)
```

Output:

[1] 8 9 16

Explanation:

(e1^e2): The first vector e1 raised to the exponent of second vector e2, then it produces the result 8,9,16.

Greater Than

```
>
```

Checks if each element of the first vector is greater than the corresponding element in the second vector.

Example 3.8

```
g1<- c(6,8,9)
g2<- c(9,2,6)
print (g1 > g2)
```

Output:

[1] FALSE TRUE TRUE

Explanation:

(g1>g2): Checks if each element of the first vector g1 is greater than the corresponding element in the second vector g2.

Less Than

```
<
```

Checks if each element of the first vector is less than the corresponding element in the second vector.

Example 3.9

```
g1<- c(6,8,9)
g2<- c(9,2,6)
print (g1 < g2)
```

Output:

[1] TRUE FALSE FALSE

Explanation:

(g1<g2): Checks if each element of the first vector g1 is less than the corresponding element in the second vector g2.

Equal To

```
==
```

Checks if each element in the first vector is equal to the corresponding element in the second vector.

Example 3.10

```
e1<- c(3,6,9)

e2<- c(2,7,9)

print(e1==e2)
```

Output:

[1] FALSE FALSE TRUE

Explanation:

(e1==e2): Checks if each element in the first vector is equal to the corresponding element in the second vector.

Greater Than or Equal To

```
>=
```

Check if each element of the first vector is greater than or equal to the corresponding element in the second vector.

Example 3.11

```
e1<- c(3,6,9)
e2<- c(2,7,9)
print(e1>=e2)
```

Output:

[1] TRUE FALSE TRUE

Explanation:

(e1)>=e2): Checks if each element in the first vector e1 is greater than or equal to the corresponding element in the second vector e2.

Less Than or Equal To

```
<=
```

Check if each element of the first vector is less than or equal to the corresponding element in the second vector.

Example 3.12

```
e1<- c(3,6,9)
e2<- c(2,7,9)
print(e1<=e2)
```

Output:

[1] FALSE TRUE TRUE

Explanation:

(e1)<=e2): Checks if each element in the first vector e1 is less than or equal to the corresponding element in the second vector e2.

Not Equal To

```
!=
```

Check if each element of the first vector is not equal to the corresponding element in the second vector.

Example 3.13

```
e1<- c(3,6,9)

e2<- c(2,7,9)

print(e1!=e2)
```

Output:

[1] TRUE TRUE FALSE

Explanation:

(e1)!=e2): Checks if each element in the first vector e1 is not equal to the corresponding element in the second vector e2.

Note: About the logical values, all numbers greater than 1 are considered to be TRUE, all numbers less than or equal to 0 are considered to be FALSE.

AND

&

Compares each element of the first vector with the corresponding element of the second vector, If both elements are TRUE, the output is TRUE.

Example 3.14

```
a1<- c(100,0,TRUE)

a2<- c(10, 20, FALSE)

print(a1&a2)
```

Output:

[1] TRUE FALSE FALSE

Explanation:

(a1&a2): compares a1 with a2, if both elements are TRUE, the output is TRUE.

OR

```
|
```

Compares each element of the first vector with the corresponding element of the second vector, If one of the elements is TRUE, the output is TRUE.

Example 3.15

```
a1<- c(100,0, FALSE)

a2<- c(10, 20, FALSE)

print(a1|a2)
```

Output:

[1] TRUE TRUE FALSE

Explanation:

(a1|a2): compares a1 with a2, If one of the elements is TRUE, the output is TRUE.

NOT

!

Gets each element of the vector and returns the opposite logical value.

Example 3.16

```
n<- c(100,0,TRUE)

print(!n)
```

Output:

[1] FALSE TRUE FALSE

Explanation:

(!n): Gets each element of the vector and returns the opposite logical value.

Logical AND

&&

Compares only the first element of both vectors, and the result will be TRUE if both are TRUE.

Example 3.17

```
a1<- c(100,0,TRUE)

a2<- c(0, 20,FALSE)

print(a1 && a2)
```

Output:

[1] FALSE

Explanation:

The meaning of the warning is: the output will have one result rather than three results if using && operator.

(a1&&a2): Only compares the first element of both vectors, and the result will be TRUE if both are TRUE.

Logical OR

```
||
```

Compares only the first element of both vectors, and the result will be TRUE if one of the elements is TRUE.

Example 3.18

```
a1<- c(100,0,TRUE)

a2<- c(0, 20,FALSE)

print(a1||a2)
```

Output:

[1] TRUE

Explanation:

The meaning of the warning is: the output will have one result rather than three results if using || operator.

(a1||a2): Only compares the first element of both vectors, and the result will be TRUE if one of the elements is TRUE.

Left Assignment

```
<- or <<-
```

<- or <<- is an operator of the left assignment.

Example 3.19

```
a1<- c(100,0,TRUE)

a2<<- c(100,0,TRUE)

print(a1)

print(a2)
```

Output:

[1] 100 0 1

[1] 100 0 1

Explanation:

<- and <<- are operators of the left assignments.

Right Assignment

-> or ->>

-> or ->> is an operator of the right assignment.

Example 3.20

```
c(100,0,TRUE) ->a1
c(100,0,TRUE) ->> a2
print(a1)
print(a2)
```

Output:

[1] 100   0   1

[1] 100   0   1

Explanation:

-> and ->> are operators of the right assignments.

Colon operator

number1 : number2

"number1: number2" creates a series of sequent numbers from number1 to number2.

Example 3.21

v <- 1:8

print(v)

Output:

[1] 1 2 3 4 5 6 7 8

Explanation:

v <- 1:8 creates a series of sequent numbers 12345678.

Member Operator

%in%

Identify whether an element belongs to a vector.

Example 3.22

```
v1 <- 6;

v2 <- 15;

m <- 1:8;

print(v1 %in% m);

print(v2 %in% m);
```

Output:

[1] TRUE

[1] FALSE

Explanation:

print(v1 %in% m): v1 belongs to m, therefore it returns true.

print(v2 %in% m): v2 doesn't belong to m, therefore it returns false.

Summary

R Language provides operators of the following types:

Arithmetic operator (+, -, *, /)

Relational operator (>, <, ==, !=, <=, >=)

Logical operator (&, ||, !)

Assignment operator (<-, <<-, ->, ->>)

Other operators (: , %in%)

"+" One vector adds another.

"-" One vector subtracts another.

"*" One vector multiplies another.

"/" The first vector divided by the second vector.

"%%" The first vector is divided by the second vector, then gets the remainder.

"%/%" The first vector divided by the second vector, then gets the modulus.

"^" The first vector is raised to the exponent of the second vector.

">" Checks if each element of the first vector is greater than the corresponding element in the second vector.

"<" Checks if each element of the first vector is less than the corresponding element in the second vector.

"==" Checks if each element in the first vector is equal to the corresponding element in the second vector.

">=" Check if each element of the first vector is greater than or equal to the corresponding element in the second vector.

"<=" Check if each element of the first vector is less than or equal to the corresponding element in the second vector.

"!=" Check if each element of the first vector is not equal to the corresponding element in the second vector.

"&" Compares each element of the first vector with the corresponding element of the second vector, If both elements are TRUE, the output is TRUE.

"|" Compares each element of the first vector with the corresponding element of the second vector, If one of the elements is TRUE, the output is TRUE.

"!" Gets each element of the vector and returns the opposite logical value.

"&&" Compares only the first element of both vectors, and the result will be TRUE if both are TRUE.

"||" Compares only the first element of both vectors, and the result will be TRUE if one of the elements is TRUE.

"<-" or "<<-" is an operator of the left assignment.

"->" or "->>"is an operator of the right assignment.

":" Creates a series of sequent numbers for the vector.

"%in%" Identifies whether an element belongs to a vector.

Chapter 4

If Statement

```
if (boolean_expression) {

statement

}
```

The statement will be executed if the boolean expression is true.

Example 4.1

```
m <- 200

n <- 100

if (m > n) {

print("m is greater than n")

}
```

Output:

[1] "m is greater than n"

Explanation:

Because m>n is true, the statement can be executed.

If...else Statement

```
if (boolean_expression) {
   Statement1
} else {
   Statement2
}
```

The statement1 will be executed if the boolean expression is true. Otherwise, the statement2 will be executed if the boolean expression is false.

Example 4.2

```
m <- 200
n <- 100
if (m < n) {
   print("m is less than n")
} else {
   print ("m is greater than n")
}
```

Output: [1] "m is greater than n"

Explanation:

Because m is greater than n, the else statement can be executed.

Switch Statement

---

variable <- value

switch(variable, case1, case2, case3....)

The value of the variable will compare each case, if equals one of the "case" value; it will execute that "case" code.

Example 4.3

---

var <- "vegetable"

switch(

var,

fruit = "apple",

vegetable = "broccoli",

meat = "chicken"

)

Output:

[1] "broccoli"

Explanation:

The value of var is "vegetable", therefore, it outputs "broccoli".

Loop

There are many regular repetitive operations in actual programming, so some statements need to be executed repeatedly in the program. A set of statements that are executed repeatedly is called a loop body, and whether or not it can be repeated is determined by the termination conditions of the loop.

There are three types of loop statement:

1. repeat loop

2. while loop

3. for loop

Repeat Loop

```
repeat {
  statements
  if(condition) {
    break
  }
}
```

The repeat loop executes the same code again and again until the stop condition is met.

Example 4.4

```
var <- c("Very Good!")

num <- 0

repeat {

  print(var)

  num <- num+1

  if(num >= 5) {

    break    # stop the loop

  }

}
```

Output:

[1] "Very Good!"

[1] "Very Good!"

[1] "Very Good!"

[1] "Very Good!"

[1] "Very Good!"

Explanation:

repeat{ } is a loop statement, when num is greater than or equal to 5, the loop is stopped.

While Loop

```
while (condition) {

  statement

}
```

The while loop will execute the same code over and over until the stop condition is met.

Example 4.5

```
var <- c("OK! Wonderful")

num <- 0

while (num < 5) {    # condition

  print(var)

  num = num + 1

}
```

Output:

[1] "OK! Wonderful"

[1] "OK! Wonderful"

[1] "OK! Wonderful"

[1] "OK! Wonderful"

[1] "OK! Wonderful"

Explanation:

while (num < 5) is a test expression, if num is less than 5, the loop will run 5 times. if num is equal to 5, the loop will stop.

The while loop will execute the same code over and over until the stop condition is met.

For Loop

```
for (value in vector) {
   statements
}
```

For loop can execute a specified number of loops.

Example 4.6

```
var =c(1:5)

num = 1

for(num in var){

  print("Excellent!")

}
```

Output:

[1] "Excellent!"

[1] "Excellent!"

[1] "Excellent!"

[1] "Excellent!"

[1] "Excellent!"

Explanation:

var =c(1:5) specifies the number of loops, let the program loop automatically five times.

Function

A function is a code block that can repeat to run many times, it is a set of statements that are grouped together to perform a specified task. R language has a number of built-in functions, and of course users can create their own functions.

1. The syntax to define a function is as follows:

```
functionName <- function(arg1, arg2, ...) {

  body

  return(object)

}
```

"functionName" is the function name.

"Arg1, arg2" are parameters.

"body" is function statement.

"return (object)" returns the result to the function caller.

2. The syntax to call the function is:

```
functionName( arg )     # this is the function caller
```

Example 4.7

```
myfunction <- function(x, y){   # define a function

num <- x+y

print(num)

}

myfunction(100,200)     # call the function
```

Output:

[1] 300

Explanation:

myfunction <- function(x, y) defines a function. x and y are arguments. myfunction(100,200) calls the function, and passes the arguments 100 and 200 to x and y.

Example 4.8

```
myfunction <- function(x, y){

num <- x+y

return(num)   # return the result to the caller

}

result=myfunction( 100, 200 )   # call the function

print(result)
```

Output:

[1] 300

Explanation:

"myfunction(100, 200)" is a function caller.

"return(num)" returns the value of num to the function caller "myfunction(100, 200)".

Just like "myfunction(100, 200) <- return(num)".

Function without Argument

The syntax of a function without argument is:

```
functionName <- function() {

  body

}
```

Example 4.9

```
myfunction <- function(){    # define a function

num <- 300+400

print(num)

}
myfunction()      # call the function
```

Output:

[1] 700

Explanation:

myfunction() calls the function without arguments, so doesn't passes any value to the function.

Function with default arguments

The syntax of a function with default arguments is:

```
functionName <- function(x=val1, y=val2) {

  body

}
```

Example 4.10

```
myfunction <- function( x=1, y=2 ){    # default arguments

num <- x+y

print(num)

}
myfunction()    # call the function
```

Output:

[1] 3

Explanation:

myfunction() calls the function with default arguments,

(x=val1, y=val2) is the default arguments.

Built-in Functions

R language has many built-in functions that users do not have to define these kinds of functions. Built-in functions can be called directly in programs.

The following are some built-in functions:

length(), sort(), substr(), max(), min(), abs(), sin()......

For Example

```
> print(sum(100, 200))    # get the sum
[1] 300
> print(abs(-1000))   # get the absolute value
[1] 1000
> print(max(100, 200))    # get the maximum
[1] 200
> print(min(100, 200))    # get the minimum
[1] 100
> print(sqrt(81))   # get the square root
[1] 9
> num <- c(2,8,5,9,3)
> print(sort(num))   # sort the numbers
[1] 2 3 5 8 9
```

String & Substring

Any values written in single or double quotes in R language will be treated as strings.

1. The syntax to declare a string is:

```
"string"

'string'
```

We can see the string is always enclosed by a pair of double quotes or a pair of single quotes.

2. The syntax to get a substring is:

```
substr("string", index1, index2)
```

substr("string", index1, index2) gets a sub string in the specified string from the index1 to index2.

For example:

> print(**substr**("JavaScript", 1, 4))   # get a substring from 1 to 4

[1] "Java"

> print(**substr**("jQuery", 2, 6))   # get a substring from 2 to 6

[1] "Query"

Convert to String

```
format(value)
```

format(value) can convert any value to a string.

Example 4.11

```
str1 <- format(100)      # convert to string

str2 <- format(200)      # convert to string

print(str1)

print(str2)
```

Output:

[1] "100"

[1] "200"

Explanation:

"100" is a string now

"200" is a string now

Connect Strings

The syntax to connect strings is:

```
paste(str1, str2, str3,...sep="separators")
```

paste(str1, str2, str3,...sep="separators") can connect some strings and become one string. The default separator is a space.

Example 4.12

```
a="C#"

b="in"

c="8"

d="Hours"

paste(a, b, c, d)     # connect four strings together
```

Output:

[1] "C# in 8 Hours"

Explanation:

paste(a, b, c, d) connects four strings.

Count Character Numbers

The syntax to count the character number in a string is:

```
nchar("string")
```

nchar("string") can calculate the number of characters in a string.

Example 4.13

```
num = nchar("Java in 8 Hours")    # count character number

print(num)
```

Output:

[1] 15

Explanation:

"Java in 8 Hours" has 15 characters

Convert to Upper Case

The syntax to convert a string to upper case is:

```
toupper()
```

toupper() can convert lower cases to upper case.

Example 4.14

```
str = "html css in 8 hours"

print(toupper(str))
```

Output:

[1] "HTML CSS IN 8 HOURS"

Explanation:

"html css in 8 hours" has been converted to upper case now.

Convert to Lower Case

The syntax to convert a string to lower case is:

```
tolower()
```

tolower() can convert upper cases to lower case.

Example 4.15

```
str = "PHP MYSQL In 8 Hours"

print(tolower(str))
```

Output:

[1] "php mysql in 8 hours"

Explanation:

"PHP MYSQL In 8 Hours" has been converted to lower case now.

Character Replacement

The syntax to replace old characters with new characters is:

```
chartr(old="v1", new="v2", str="string")
```

chartr(old="v1", new="v2", str="string") can replace old characters with new characters in a string.

Example 4.16

```
str = (chartr(old="Html", new="Ruby", "Html in 8 Hours"))
print (str)
```

Output:

[1] "Ruby in 8 Hours"

Explanation:

The old characters "Html" has been replaced by the new characters "Ruby".

Summary

The syntax of If Statement:

if(boolean_expression) {

} else {

}

The syntax of Switch Statement:

variable <- value

switch(variable, case1, case2, case3....)

The syntax of Repeat Loop:

repeat {

  statements

  if(condition) {

    break

  }

}

The syntax of While Loop:

while (condition) {

  statement

}

The syntax of For Loop:

for (value in vector) {

}

Declare a Function:

```
functionName <- function(arg1, arg2, ...) {

    body

    return(object)

}
```

Call the Function:

functionName()

Built-in functions:

length(), sort(), substr(), max(), min(), abs(), sin()......

The quotes at the beginning and the end of the string should be single or double quotes: "string" or 'string'.

substr("string", index1, index2) gets a sub string in the specified string from the index1 to index2.

format(value) can convert any value to a string.

paste(str1, str2, str3,...sep="separators") can connect some strings and become one string. The default separator is a space.

nchar("string") can calculate the number of characters in a string.

toupper() can convert lower cases to upper case.

tolower() can convert upper cases to lower case.

chartr(old="v1", new="v2", str="string") can replace old characters with new characters in a string.

Chapter 5

Vector

In R language, vectors are the most essential objects. There are six types of vectors, which are character, integer, double, logical, complex, and raw vector.

A value is considered to be a vector; its length is 1.

1. The following examples show how to create one element vector.

For example:

> print("good")   # "good" is a character vector

[1] "good"

print(20.8)   # 20.8 is a double vector

[1] 20.8

print(68L)   # 68L is an integer vector

[1] 68L

print(FALSE)   # FALSE is a logical vector

[1] FALSE

print(3+2i)   # 3+2i is a complex vector

[1] 3+2i

print(charToRaw('Excellent'))   # convert to a raw vector

[1] 45 78 63 65 6c 6c 65 6e 74

2. The following examples show how to create a multiple element vector using colon operator.

For example:

> print(2:8)   # using colon operator

[1] 2 3 4 5 6 7 8

> print(1.8 : 6.8)   # using colon operator

[1] 1.8 2.8 3.8 4.8 5.8 6.8

3. The following example shows how to create a multiple element vector by using c( ).

For example:

> print(c(3,4,5))   # using c( )

[1] 3 4 5

> print(**c**("apple", "banana", "cherry"))   # using c( )

[1] "apple" "banana" "cherry"

sep( ) function

The syntax to create a vector from v1 to v2 is:

```
seq(v1, v2,  by = step)
```

seq(v1, v2, by = step) can create a vector from v1 to v2.

by = step specifies the distance among each element.

Example 5.1

```
print(seq(10, 50, by = 5))
```

Output:

[1] 10 15 20 25 30 35 40 45 50

Explanation:

seq(10, 50, by = 5) creates a vector from 10 to 50, its step is 5.

Access the Vector (1)

The syntax to access the specified element in a vector is:

```
c( index )
```

"index" is used to specify an element that will be accessed.

The index starts with 1.

TRUE, FALSE, 1,0 , and all numbers can work as an index.

Example 5.2

```
v <- c("apple", "banana", "cherry", "durian")
print(v[c(1,3)])
```

Output:

[1] "apple" "cherry"

Explanation:

v[c(1,3)]) accesses the elements with index 1 and index 3.

Access the Vector (2)

The syntax to access the specified element in a vector is:

c(TRUE)   # the corresponding element will be accessed

c(FALSE)   # the corresponding element won't be accessed

TRUE, FALSE can work as an index.

Example 5.3

```
v <- c("apple", "banana", "cherry", "durian")
print(v[c(FALSE, TRUE, FALSE, TRUE)])
```

Output:

[1] "banana" "durian"

Explanation:

v[c(FALSE,TRUE,FALSE,TRUE)] only accesses the elements with index TRUE.

Delete Vector Element

The syntax to remove a specified element is:

```
c( -index )
```

Assigning a negative value to an index can remove the corresponding element.

Example 5.4

```
v <- c("apple", "banana", "cherry", "Durian")
print( v[c(-2,-4)] )   # remove the 2nd and the 4th element
```

Output:

[1] "apple" "cherry"

Explanation:

v[c(-2,-4)] removes the elements with index -2 and index -4.

Vector Addition

The syntax of the vector addition is:

```
vector1+ vector2
```

All elements in vector1 add all corresponding elements in vector2.

Example 5.5

```
v1 <- c(1,2,3)

v2 <- c(4,5,6)

print(v1+v2)
```

Output:

[1] 5 7 9

Explanation:

All elements in vector1 add all corresponding elements in vector2.

Vector Subtraction

The syntax of the vector subtraction is:

```
vector1 - vector2
```

All elements in vector1 add all corresponding elements in vector2.

Example 5.6

```
v1 <- c(7,8,9)

v2 <- c(2,6,3)

print(v1-v2)
```

Output:

[1] 5 2 6

Explanation:

All elements in vector1 subtract all corresponding elements in vector2.

Vector Multiplication

The syntax of the vector multiplication is:

vector1 * vector2

All elements in vector1 add all corresponding elements in vector2.

Example 5.7

```
v1 <- c(7,8,9)

v2 <- c(2,6,3)

print( v1*v2 )
```

Output:

[1] 14 48 27

Explanation:

All elements in vector1 multiply all corresponding elements in vector2.

Vector Division

The syntax of the vector division is:

```
vector1 / vector2
```

All elements in vector1 divide all corresponding elements in vector2.

Example 5.8

```
v1 <- c(16,27,32)
v2 <- c(8,3,4)
print(v1/v2)
```

Output:

[1] 2 9 8

Explanation:

All elements in vector1 divide all corresponding elements in vector2.

Vector of Different Length

If two vector lengths are different as follows:

```
v1 <- c(a, b, c, d, e, f)
v2 <- c(x, y)
```

When two vectors of different lengths are manipulated, shorter vectors are treated as equal lengths.

v2 will become c(x, y, x, y, x, y) for matching v1

Example 5.9

```
v1 <- c(4,5,6,7,8,9)

v2 <- c(2,3)    # v2 becomes c(2,3,2,3,2,3)

result <- (v1+ v2)

print(result)
```

Output:

[1] 6 8 8 10 10 12

Explanation:

v2 <- c(2,3) is treated as c(2,3,2,3,2,3) for matching v1.

Let's study one more example as follows:

Example 5.10

```
v1 <- c(4,5,6,7,8,9)
v2 <- c(2,3)      # v2 becomes c(2,3,2,3,2,3)
result <- (v1 - v2)
print(result)
```

Output:

[1] 2 2 4 4 6 6

Explanation:

v2 <- c(2,3) is treated as c(2,3,2,3,2,3) for matching v1.

Sorting Vector

The syntax to sort a vector is as follows:

```
sort( vector, decreasing=TRUE/FALSE)
```

"decreasing=TRUE/FALSE" specifies ascending order or descending order.

Example 5.11

```
v <- c(2, 18, 7, 35, 0, 11, -16, 100)
result <- sort(v, decreasing=FALSE)
print(result)
```

Output:

[1] -16 0 2 7 11 18 35 100

Explanation:

"decreasing=FALSE" specifies ascending order to sort the vector elements.

Let's study one more example as follows:

Example 5.12

```
v <- c(2,18,7,35,0,11,-16,100)

result <- sort(v, decreasing=TRUE)

print(result)
```

Output:

[1] 100 35 18 11   7   2   0 -16

Explanation:

"decreasing=TRUE" specifies descending order to sort the vector elements.

List

List is an R object that contains elements of different types, such as numbers, strings, and vectors.

Lists are created by using the list() function.

The syntax to create a list is:

```
list(val1, val2, val3, ...)
```

list(val1, val2, val3, ...) can create a list.

val1, val2, val3, can be strings, numbers, vectors and logical values.

Example 5.13

```
myList <- list("apple", "banana", "cherry", "durian");

print(myList)
```

Output:

[[1]]
[1] "apple"

[[2]]
[1] "banana"

[[3]]
[1] "cherry"

[[4]]
[1] "durian"

Explanation:

list("apple", "banana", "cherry", "durian") creates a list with four elements.

Access the Elements of List

The syntax to access the elements of list is:

```
myList[index]
```

myList[index] can access a specified element in the list.

"index" starts with 1.

Example 5.14

```
myList <- list("apple", "banana", "cherry", "durian");

print(myList[3])
```

Output:

[1] "cherry"

Explanation:

myList[3] accesses the third element in the list.

Add an Element to List

The syntax to add an Element at the end of the list is:

```
myList[lastIndex] <- "New element"
```

Example 5.15

```
myList <- list("apple", "banana", "cherry", "durian")
myList[5] <- "egg-fruit"
print(myList)
```

Output:

[[1]]
[1] "apple"
[[2]]
[1] "banana"
[[3]]
[1] "cherry"
[[4]]
[1] "durian"
[[5]]
[1] "egg-fruit"

Explanation: myList[5] <- "egg-fruit" adds an element "egg-fruit" to the index 5 in myList.

Remove the Last Element

The syntax to remove the last element of the list is:

```
myList[lastIndex] <- NULL
```

Remove an element at the end of the list.

Example 5.16

```
myList <- list("A", "B", "C", "D")

myList[4] <- NULL

print(myList)
```

Output:

[[1]]
[1] "A"
[[2]]
[1] "B"
[[3]]
[1] "C"

Explanation:

myList[4] <- NULL removes the element at index 4 in myList.

Update an Element

The syntax to update an element of a list is:

```
myList[Index] <- "New element"
```

Update a specified element in the list.

Example 5.17

```
myList <- list("apple", "banana", "cherry", "durian")

myList[3] <- "chestnut"    # replace "cherry"

print(myList)
```

Output:

[[1]]
[1] "apple"
[[2]]
[1] "banana"
[[3]]
[1] "chestnut"
[[4]]
[1] "durian"

Explanation:

myList[3] <- "chestnut" updates the element at index 3 in myList.

Merge Two Lists

The syntax to merge two lists is:

```
myList <- c(list1, list2)
```

c(list1, list2) can merge two lists into one list.

Example 5.18

```
list1 <- list("apple", "banana", "cherry", "durian")

list2 <- list("A", "B", "C", "D")

myList <- c(list1, list2)

print(myList)
```

Output:

[[1]]

[1] "apple"

[[2]]

[1] "banana"

[[3]]

[1] "cherry"

[[4]]

[1] "durian"

[[5]]

[1] "A"

[[6]]

[1] "B"

[[7]]

[1] "C"

[[8]]

[1] "D"

Explanation:

c(list1, list2) merges two lists into one list.

Convert List to Vector

The syntax to convert a list to a vector is:

unlist( )

unlist( ) can convert a list to a vector.

(Please restart RGui before running the following program)

Example 5.19

```
myList <- list(2:6)    # create a list

print(myList)

myVector <- unlist(myList)    # convert to vector

print(myVector)
```

Output

[[1]]

[1] 2 3 4 5 6

[1] 2 3 4 5 6

Explanation:

myVector <- **unlist**(myList) converts a list to a vector.

Summary

In R, a value is considered to be a vector; its length is 1.

The example to create one element vector:

> print("good")   # "good" is a character vector

[1] "good"

The example to create a multiple element vector:

> print(2:8)

[1] 2 3 4 5 6 7 8

> print(c(3,4,5))

[1] 3 4 5

seq(v1, v2, by = step) can create a vector from v1 to v2.

by = step specifies the distance among each element.

[index] can access all elements of a vector, the index starts with 1.

TRUE, FALSE, 1,0 , and all numbers can work as an index.

[-index] Assigning a negative value to an index can remove the corresponding element.

When two vectors of different lengths are manipulated, shorter vectors are treated as equal lengths.

"sort(vector, decreasing=TRUE/FALSE)" sorts elements in a vector.

list(val1, val2, val3, ...) can create a list.

"myList[index]" can access a specified element in the list.

"index" starts with 1.

myList[lastIndex] <- "New element" adds an element at the end of the list.

myList[lastIndex] <- NULL removes an element at the end of the list.

myList[Index] <- "New element" updates a specified element in the list.

c(list1, list2) can merge two lists into one list.

unlist( ) can convert a list to a vector.

Chapter 6

Matrix

A matrix is a two-dimensional array formed by the data with length and width. Its units must be the same data type. Columns represent different variables and rows represent every object. Matrices can be used for mathematical calculations.

The syntax to create a Matrix is:

matrix(data, nrow, ncol, byrow, dimnames)

"data" is the matrix elements.

"nrow" is the number of rows.

"ncol" is the number of columns.

"byrow" is an arrangement. If TRUE, the elements are arranged by row, If FALSE, the elements are arranged by column. The default value is FALSE.

"dimnames" is the names of the rows and columns.

Example 6.1

```
myMatrix <- matrix(c(1:20), nrow = 5, byrow = TRUE)

print(myMatrix)
```

Output:

	[,1]	[,2]	[,3]	[,4]
[1,]	1	2	3	4
[2,]	5	6	7	8
[3,]	9	10	11	12
[4,]	13	14	15	16
[5,]	17	18	19	20

Explanation:

"**matrix**(c(1:20)" creates a matrix containing 20 elements.

"nrow = 5" specifies that the number of rows is 5.

"byrow = TRUE" specifies that matrix is arranged by row.

Let's study one more example as follows:

Example 6.2

myMatrix <- **matrix**(c(1:18), ncol = 6, byrow = FALSE)

print(myMatrix)

Output:

```
     [,1] [,2] [,3] [,4] [,5] [,6]
[1,]   1    4    7   10   13   16
[2,]   2    5    8   11   14   17
[3,]   3    6    9   12   15   18
```

Explanation:

"**matrix**(c(1:18)" creates a matrix containing 18 elements.

ncol = 6 specifies that the number of columns is 6.

Byrow = FALSE specifies the matrix is arranged by column.

(The example on the next page will show how to access the element of this matrix.)

Access the Matrix

The syntax to access the matrix is as follows:

myMatrix[row, column]

myMatrix[row, column] can access the matrix's elements according to row and column.

Example 6.3

```
myMatrix <- matrix(c(1:18), ncol = 6, byrow = FALSE)

print(myMatrix)

print(myMatrix[2,3])     # access the Matrix
```

Output:

 [1] 8

Explanation:

myMatrix[2,3] accesses the element at row 2 and column 3.

Let's study one more example as follows:

Example 6.4

```
myMatrix <- matrix(c(1:18), ncol = 6, byrow = FALSE)

print(myMatrix)

print(myMatrix[3,6])    # access the Matrix
```

Output:

[1] 18

Explanation:

myMatrix[3,6] accesses the element at row 3 and column 6.

Creating Matrices

Example 6.5

```
matrix1 <- matrix(c(4, 5, 6, 7, 8, 9), nrow = 2)

print(matrix1)
```

Output:

```
      [,1]  [,2]  [,3]
[1,]    4     6     8
[2,]    5     7     9
```

Explanation:

"**matrix**(c(4, 5, 6, 7, 8, 9), nrow = 2)" creates a matrix containing elements from 4 to 9, and 2 rows.

Let's study one more example as follows:

Example 6.6

---

matrix2 <- **matrix**(c(2, 8, 3, 1, 6, 7), nrow = 2)

print(matrix2)

Output:

```
      [,1] [,2] [,3]
[1,]   2    3    6
[2,]   8    1    7
```

Explanation:

"**matrix**(c(2, 8, 3, 1, 6, 7), nrow = 2)" creates a matrix containing elements from 1 to 8, and 2 rows.

Matrix Addition

The syntax of matrix addition is:

matrix1+ matrix2

Example 6.7

matrix1 and matrix2 comes from the above examples.

```
matrix1 <- matrix(c(4, 5, 6, 7, 8, 9), nrow = 2)
matrix2 <- matrix(c(2, 8, 3, 1, 6, 7), nrow = 2)
myMatrix <- matrix1 + matrix2
print(myMatrix)
```

Output:

```
     [,1] [,2] [,3]
[1,]   6    9   14
[2,]  13    8   16
```

Explanation:

"matrix1 + matrix2" means that the elements at matrix1 adds the corresponding elements in matrix2.

Matrix Subtraction

The syntax of matrix subtraction is:

matrix1 – matrix2

Example 6.8

matrix1 and matrix2 comes from the above examples.

```
matrix1 <- matrix(c(4, 5, 6, 7, 8, 9), nrow = 2)

matrix2 <- matrix(c(2, 8, 3, 1, 6, 7), nrow = 2)

myMatrix <- matrix1 - matrix2

print(myMatrix)
```

Output:

```
      [,1] [,2] [,3]
[1,]    2    3    2
[2,]   -3    6    2
```

Explanation:

"matrix1 - matrix2" means that the elements at matrix1 subtracts the corresponding elements in matrix2.

Matrix Multiplication

The syntax of matrix multiplication is:

matrix1 * matrix2

Example 6.9

matrix1 and matrix2 comes from the above examples.

```
matrix1 <- matrix(c(4, 5, 6, 7, 8, 9), nrow = 2)

matrix2 <- matrix(c(2, 8, 3, 1, 6, 7), nrow = 2)

myMatrix <- matrix1 * matrix2

print(myMatrix)
```

Output:

```
      [,1] [,2] [,3]
[1,]    8   18   48
[2,]   40    7   63
```

Explanation:

"matrix1 * matrix2" means that the elements at matrix1 multiplies the corresponding elements in matrix2.

Matrix Division

The syntax of matrix division is:

matrix1 / matrix2

Example 6.10

matrix1 and matrix2 comes from the above examples.

matrix1 <- matrix(c(4, 5, 6, 7, 8, 9), nrow = 2)

matrix2 <- matrix(c(2, 8, 3, 1, 6, 7), nrow = 2)

myMatrix <- **matrix1 / matrix2**

print(myMatrix)

Output:

```
      [,1] [,2]    [,3]
[1,] 2.000    2 1.333333
[2,] 0.625    7 1.285714
```

Explanation:

"matrix1 / matrix2" means that the elements at matrix1 divides the corresponding elements in matrix2.

Name Rows & Columns

The syntax to name the row and column is:

dimnames = list(rownames, colnames)

list(rownames, colnames) defines the names for each row and column.

Example 6.11

```
rn = c("row1", "row2", "row3" )    # set three row names

cn = c("col1", "col2", "col3", "col4")    # set four column names

myMatrix <- matrix(c(1:12), nrow = 3, dimnames = list(rn, cn))

print(myMatrix)
```

Output:

```
      col1 col2 col3 col4
row1    1    4    7   10
row2    2    5    8   11
row3    3    6    9   12
```

Explanation:

dimnames = list(rn, cn) names the rows and columns in the matrix.

"rn" is a variable of the row name.

"cn" is a variable of the column name.

row1, row2, row3 are the names of each row.

col1, col2, col3, col4 are the names of each column.

Array

An array is a collection of elements with same type indexes.

Vector is a one-dimensional array;

Matrix is a two-dimensional array;

Array is a three-dimensional array;

Array is an extension of a matrix, it extends the matrix beyond two-dimensions.

The array element type in the R language is the same; the data type can be numeric, logical, character, or complex.

The syntax to create an array is:

```
array( data, dim, dimnames)
```

"array(data, dim, dimnames)" can create an array.

"data" is the element that creates the array.

"dim" is the dimension of an array.

"dimnames" is the tag name of each dimension.

About argument "dim", for example: dim=c(4, 3, 2) means that the array will be 4 rows, 3 columns, 2 matrices.

1. Create a one-dimensional array

Example 6.12

```
print(array(1:8))
```

like a one-dimensional vector

Output:

[1] 1 2 3 4 5 6 7 8

Explanation:

This is an array containing 8 elements.

"**array**(1:8)" creates an array containing elements from 1 to 8.

2. Create a two-dimensional array

Example 6.13

```
print(array(1:8, dim=c(2,4)))
```

like a two-dimensional matrix

Output:

```
     [,1] [,2] [,3] [,4]
[1,]   1    3    5    7
[2,]   2    4    6    8
```

Explanation:

This is an array of 2 rows & 4 columns

"**array**(1:8, dim=c(2,4))" creates a two-dimensional array containing 8 elements, 2 rows, 4 columns.

3. Create a three-dimensional array

Example 6.14

print(**array**(1:24, dim=c(2,4,3)))

create an array containing 2 rows, 4 columns, 3 matrices.

Output:

```
, , 1
      [,1] [,2] [,3] [,4]
[1,]    1    3    5    7
[2,]    2    4    6    8

, , 2
      [,1] [,2] [,3] [,4]
[1,]    9   11   13   15
[2,]   10   12   14   16

, , 3
      [,1] [,2] [,3] [,4]
[1,]   17   19   21   23
[2,]   18   20   22   24
```

Explanation:

"**array**(1:24, dim=c(2,4,3))" creates an array containing 24 elements, 2 rows, 4 columns, 3 matrixes.

Name the Array

The syntax to name an array is:

```
dimnames = list(rowname, colname, matrixname)
```

dimnames = list(rowname, colname, matrixname) defines the name of each row, each column, and each matrix in the array.

Example 6.15

```
rn <- c("Row1", "Row2", "Row3")    # set row name

cn <- c("Col1", "Col2", "Col3")    # set column name

mn <- c("Matrix1","Matrix2")    # set matrix name

arr <- array(1:18, dim=c(3,3,2), dimnames = list(rn, cn, mn))

print(arr)
```

Output:

```
, , Matrix1
     Col1 Col2 Col3
Row1    1    4    7
Row2    2    5    8
Row3    3    6    9

, , Matrix2
     Col1 Col2 Col3
Row1   10   13   16
Row2   11   14   17
Row3   12   15   18
```

Explanation:

dimnames = list(rn, cn, mn) names the each row, each column, and each matrix in the array.

"rn" is a variable of the row name.

"cn" is a variable of the column name.

"mn" is a variable of matrix name.

Row1, Row2, and Row3 are the row name.

Col1, Col2, and Col3 are the column names.

Matrix1 and Matrix2 are the matrix names.

Access Array (1)

The syntax to access an array is:

```
myArray[ x, y, z ]
```

X represents the number of the row.

Y represents the number of the column.

Z represents the number of the matrix.

Example 6.16

```
rn <- c("Row1", "Row2", "Row3")
cn <- c("Col1", "Col2", "Col3")
mn <- c("Matrix1","Matrix2")
arr <- array(1:18, dim=c(3,3,2), dimnames = list(rn, cn, mn))
print(arr)    # print the array
print(arr[2,3,1])    # access the array
```

Output:

```
, , Matrix1
     Col1 Col2 Col3
Row1    1    4    7
Row2    2    5    8
Row3    3    6    9

, , Matrix2
     Col1 Col2 Col3
Row1   10   13   16
Row2   11   14   17
Row3   12   15   18
```

[1] 8

Explanation:

"array(1:18, dim=c(3,3,2)" creates an array with 18 elements, 3 rows, 3 columns, 2 matrixes.

"dimnames = list(rn, cn, mn)" names the rows, columns, matrixes.

"**arr[2,3,1]**" accesses the array at the 2nd row, the 3rd column, and the 1st matrix.

Access Array (2)

The syntax to access an array is:

```
myArray[ x, , z ]     # note: the column is missing
```

"myArray[x, , z]" accesses all elements at the x row, z matrix.

For example:

myArray[1, , 3] access all elements at the 1st row, the 3rd matrix of myArray.

Example 6.17

```
rn <- c("Row1", "Row2", "Row3")

cn <- c("Col1", "Col2", "Col3")

mn <- c("Matrix1","Matrix2")

arr <- array(1:18, dim=c(3,3,2), dimnames = list(rn, cn, mn))

print(arr)    # print the array

print(arr[3, ,2])     # note: the column is missing
```

Output:

```
, , Matrix1
     Col1 Col2 Col3
Row1   1    4    7
Row2   2    5    8
Row3   3    6    9

, , Matrix2
     Col1 Col2 Col3
Row1   10   13   16
Row2   11   14   17
Row3   12   15   18


     Col1 Col2 Col3
      12   15   18
```

Explanation:

"**arr[3, ,2]**" accesses all elements in the 3rd row, the 2nd matrix.

Access Array (3)

The syntax to access an array is:

```
myArray[ , , z ]    # note: the row, column is missing
```

"myArray[, , z]" accesses all elements in the z matrix.

For example:

myArray[, , 3] access all elements in the 3rd matrix of myArray.

Example 6.18

```
rn <- c("Row1", "Row2", "Row3")

cn <- c("Col1", "Col2", "Col3")

mn <- c("Matrix1","Matrix2")

arr <- array(1:18, dim=c(3,3,2), dimnames = list(rn, cn, mn))

print(arr)    # print the array

print(arr[ , ,2])    # note: the row, column is missing
```

Output:

```
, , Matrix1
     Col1 Col2 Col3
Row1   1    4    7
Row2   2    5    8
Row3   3    6    9

, , Matrix2
     Col1 Col2 Col3
Row1   10   13   16
Row2   11   14   17
Row3   12   15   18


     Col1 Col2 Col3
Row1   10   13   16
Row2   11   14   17
Row3   12   15   18
```

Explanation:

"**arr[, ,2]**" accesses all elements in the 2nd matrix.

Array Calculation

The syntax to calculate an array is:

---

apply(myArray, c(number), function)

---

apply( ): calculate the array's elements.

c(1): calculate the row elements.

c(2): calculate the column elements,

c(3): calculate elements in both row and column.

function: built-in functions such as sum, max , min, sort...

Example 6.19

1. Create an array

---

vector1 <- c(1,2,3)

vector2 <- c(4,5,6,7,8,9)

myArray <- **array(c(vector1,vector2)**,dim = c(3,3,1))

print(myArray)   # create an array "myArray"

Output:

```
, , 1

     [,1] [,2] [,3]
[1,]   1    4    7
[2,]   2    5    8
[3,]   3    6    9
```

Explanation:

"array(c(vector1,vector2),dim = c(3,3,1))" creates an array with 9 elements, 3 rows, 3 columns, 1 matrix.

2. Use apply() to calculate the sum of the rows

```
result1 <- apply(myArray, c(1), sum)

print(result1)    # sum is a built-in function
```

Output: [1] 12 15 18

Explanation: c(1) means to calculate the row elements.

3. Use apply() to calculate the sum of the columns

```
result2 <- apply(myArray, c(2), sum)

print(result2)    # sum is a built-in function
```

Output: [1] 6 15 24

Explanation: c(2) means to calculate the column elements.

4. Use apply() to sort the array elements

```
result3 <- apply(myArray, c(3), sort)

print(result3)    # sort is a built-in function
```

Output:

```
        [,1]
[1,]     1
[2,]     2
[3,]     3
[4,]     4
[5,]     5
[6,]     6
[7,]     7
[8,]     8
[9,]     9
```

Explanation:

apply( ) can operate the array's elements with function sum, max, min, sort......

c(3) means to sort elements of both row and column.

Summary

matrix(data, nrow, ncol, byrow, dimnames) creates a matrix.

myMatrix[row, column] can access the matrix's elements by row and column.

"matrix1 + matrix2" means that the elements at matrix1 adds the corresponding elements in matrix2.

"matrix1 - matrix2" means that the elements at matrix1 subtract the corresponding elements in matrix2.

"matrix1 * matrix2" means that the elements at matrix1 multiplies the corresponding elements in matrix2.

"matrix1 / matrix2" means that the elements at matrix1 divides the corresponding elements in matrix2.

list(rownames, colnames) defines the names for each row and column.

"array(data, dim, dimnames)" can create an array.

dimnames = list(rowname, colname, matrixname) defines the name of each row, each column, and each matrix in the array.

myArray[x, y, z] accesses an array

"apply(myArray, c(number), function)" calculates an array.

Chapter 7

Factor

Factors are used to store categorical variables and ordered variables, which cannot be computed but can only be classified or counted.

A factor represents a categorical variable. Sometimes a factor is considered a symbol or a number. For example, the number of people can be 1,2,3,4,5..., So the factors are 1,2,3,4,5.... And the high, medium, low at the level are also factors.

The syntax to create a factor object is:

```
factor(data, levels, labels, ...)    # create a factor object
```

"data" is the elements of a vector, such as 1:10, c("a", "b", "c").

"levels" is the same category of the elements,

 for example: (a,a,a,b,b,c,c,c,c) has three levels a, b, c.

 Each value of "levels'" is unique in factor.

"labels" is the names of the vector elements, such as "A" , "B", "C".

Example 7.1

```
myfactor=factor(1:5, levels=1:8)  # create a factor
print(myfactor)    # data from 1 to 5, unique values from 1 to 8
```

Output:

[1] 1 2 3 4 5

Levels: 1 2 3 4 5 6 7 8

Example 7.2

```
data= 1:5    # data from 1 to 5,

myfactor=factor(data, levels=1:3)    # create a factor

print(myfactor)    # unique values from 1 to 3
```

Output:

[1] 1   2   3   <NA> <NA>

Levels: 1 2 3

Example 7.3

```
data <- c("A","C","B","B", "C","A")   # data: A, C, B, B, C, A

myfactor=factor(data)    # create a factor

print(myfactor)   # default levels: the unique values of data
```

Output:

[1] A C B B C A

Levels: A B C

Example 7.4

```
myfactor = factor(1:5,    # data from 1 to 5

levels=1:8,    # unique values from  "1" to "8"

labels=c("a", "b", "c", "d", "e", "f", "g", "h"))    # new names

print(myfactor)
```

Output:

[1] a b c d e

Levels: a b c d e f g h

Example 7.5

```
myfactor = factor(1:5,    # data from 1 to 5

levels=1:3,    # unique values from  "1" to "3"

labels=c("a", "b", "c"))    # new name from "a" to "c"

print(myfactor)
```

Output:

[1] a   b   c   <NA> <NA>

Levels: a b c

Example 7.6

```
data <- c("A","B","C","C", "B","A")

myfactor = factor(data,      # data from A to C

labels=c("apple", "banana", "cherry"))     # new names

print(myfactor)    # default levels: the unique value of data
```

Output:

[1] apple banana cherry cherry banana apple

Levels: apple banana cherry

Explanation:

factor() can create a factor object.

"data" is the elements of a vector, such as 1:10, c("a", "b", "c").

"levels" is the same category of the elements,

 for example: (a,a,a,b,b,c,c,c,c) has three levels a, b, c.

 Each value of "levels'" is unique in factor.

"labels" is the names of the vector elements, such as "A" , "B", "C".

Set Level Sequence

The syntax to specify the level sequence is:

```
levels = c( "new1","new2","new3", ... )
```

"levels = c("new1","new2","new3", ...)" can specify new the level sequence.

Example 7.7

```
myfactor=factor(c("A", "B", "C"),

levels=c("C", "B", "A"))    # set level sequence:  C, B, A

print(myfactor)
```

Output:

[1] A B C

Levels: C B A

Explanation:

"levels = c("new1","new2","new3", ...)" can specify the level order.

Let's study one more example as follows:

Example 7.8

```
data <- c("C","B","A")
myfactor = factor(data,
levels=c("A", "B", "C"))     # set new level sequence
print(myfactor)
```

Output:

[1] C B A

Levels: A B C

Explanation:

"levels=c("A", "B", "C"))" specifies the new level sequence as

" A, B, C ".

Generate Level

```
gl(n, r, labels)
```

gl(n, k, labels) can generate a factor level.

n: the number of the levels.

r: the repeated number of each level.

labels: the name of the levels.

Example 7.9

```
L <- gl(4, 2, labels = c("A", "B","C", "D"))

print(L)
```

Output:

[1] A A B B C C D D

Levels: A B C D

Explanation:

"4" specifies the number of levels as "4".

"2" specifies the repeated number of each level as "2".

"labels = c("A", "B","C", "D")" sets the name of the levels.

Let's study one more example as follows:

Example 7.10

```
L <- gl(2, 5, labels = c("A", "B"))

print(L)
```

Output:

[1] A A A A A B B B B B

Levels: A B

Explanation

"2" specifies the number of levels as "2".

"5" specifies the repeated number of each level as "5".

"labels = c("A", "B")" sets the name of the levels as A, B.

Data Frames

A data frame is a list of categories called "data.frame";

Data frames are treated as matrices that have different patterns and properties in each column.

Data frames are displayed as matrices, and selected rows or columns are indexed as matrices.

The feature of data frames:

The column names should not be empty.

The row names must be unique.

The data type can be numeric, factor, or character.

Each column must include the same number of data.

The syntax to create a data frame is:

```
myFrame =
data.frame(col1=c(), col2=c(), col3=c(), stringsAsFactors)
```

"data.frame( )" creates a data frame.

"col1, col2, col3" are the names of each column.

"stringsAsFactors= TRUE / FALSE" sets whether the strings should be converted to factors or not.

Example 7.11

Create the data frame.

```
myFrame <- data.frame(    # create a data frame

id = c(1:5),    # column1

name = c("Andy","Rose","Macy","Dany","Judy"),   # column2

score = c(85,99,95,92,96),    # column3

year = c("2009", "2002", "2008", "2006","2007"),   # column4

stringsAsFactors = FALSE

)

print(myFrame)
```

Output:

```
  id name score year

1  1 Andy    85 2009

2  2 Rose    99 2002

3  3 Macy    95 2008

4  4 Dany    92 2006

5  5 Judy    96 2007
```

Explanation:

data.frame( ) creates a data frame.

"id, name, sore, and year" are the names of each column.

"stringsAsFactors= FALSE " sets that the string is not a factor.

We will study the data frame structure in the next page.

Data Frame Structure

The syntax to display the frame structure is:

```
str(myFrame )
```

The str() function can show the structure of the data frames.

Example 7.12

Create the data frame.

```
myFrame <- data.frame(     # create a data frame

id = c(1:5),      # column1

name = c("Andy","Rose","Macy","Dany","Judy"),  # column2

score = c(85,99,95,92,96),   # column3

year = c("2009", "2002", "2008", "2006","2007"),  # column4

stringsAsFactors = FALSE

)

str(myFrame)    # show the structure of the data frame
```

Output:

'data.frame':   5 obs. of 4 variables:

 $ id   : int 1 2 3 4 5

 $ name : chr "Andy" "Rose" "Macy" "Dany" ...

 $ score: num 85 99 95 92 96

 $ year : chr "2009" "2002" "2008" "2006" ...

Explanation:

The str() function can display the structure of the data frames.

The structure of data frame includes column names, data types, data items......

Summary of Data Frames

The syntax to show the summary of the data frame is:

```
summary(myFrame )
```

summary( ) can provide the values of the minimum, maximum, quartile, length, class, mode and numeric variables, as well as the frequency statistics of the factor vector and logical vector.

Example 7.13

Create the data frame.

```
myFrame <- data.frame(

id = c(1:5),

name = c("Andy","Rose","Macy","Dany","Judy"),

score = c(85,99,95,92,96),

year = c("2009", "2002", "2008", "2006","2007"),

stringsAsFactors = FALSE

)

summary(myFrame)   # show the summary of the data frame
```

Output:

```
         id            name                score              year
 Min.    :1    Length:5           Min.    :85.0    Length:5
 1st Qu.:2     Class :character   1st Qu.:92.0     Class :character
 Median :3     Mode  :character   Median :95.0     Mode  :character
 Mean   :3                        Mean   :93.4
 3rd Qu.:4                        3rd Qu.:96.0
 Max.   :5                        Max.   :99.0
```

Explanation:

summary( ) shows the five column name: id, name score, year,

shows the id of 12345, and shows the minimum, median,

maximum values, shows the length, class, and mode values......

Show Column Data

The syntax to specify a column data is:

```
myFrame $ column
```

"myFrame $ column" can select the data of a column.

Example 7.14

Create the data frame.

```
myFrame <- data.frame(
id = c(1:5),
name = c("Andy","Rose","Macy","Dany","Judy"),
score = c(85,99,95,92,96),
year = c("2009", "2002", "2008", "2006", "2007"),
stringsAsFactors = FALSE
)
# specify two column data
result <- data.frame(myFrame$name, myFrame$score)
print(result)
```

Output:

	myFrame.name	myFrame.score
1	Andy	85
2	Rose	99
3	Macy	95
4	Dany	92
5	Judy	96

Explanation:

"myFrame$name, myFrame$score" selects the data in two columns: name and score.

Summary

"factor(data, levels, labels, ...)" can create a factor object.

"levels = c("new1","new2","new3", ...)" can specify the level order.

gl(n, k, labels) can generate factors by specifying the pattern of their levels.

data.frame( ) can create a data frame.

The str() function can view the structure of the data frames.

summary( ) can provide the values of the minimum, maximum, quartile, length, class, mode and numeric variables, as well as the frequency statistics of the factor vector and logical vector.

"myFrame $ column" can select the specified column data.

Chapter 8

Add Columns to Data Frame

The syntax to add a column to data frame is:

myFrame $ newColumn

"myFrame $ newColumn" can add columns to a data frame.

Example 8.1

Create a data frame first, then add a column.

```
myFrame <- data.frame(
id = c(1:5),
name = c("Andy","Rose","Macy","Dany","Judy"),
score = c(85,99,95,92,96),
year = c("2009", "2002", "2008", "2006", "2007"),
stringsAsFactors = FALSE
)
# add a column named "country" to the data frame
myFrame$country <- c("US", "IN", "JP", "NZ", "CN")
result <- myFrame
print(result)
```

Output:

	id	name	score	year	country
1	1	Andy	85	2009	US
2	2	Rose	99	2002	IN
3	3	Macy	95	2008	JP
4	4	Dany	92	2006	NZ
5	5	Judy	96	2007	CN

Explanation:

"myFrame$country <- c("US", "IN", "JP", "NZ", "CN")" adds a new column named "country" to the data frame.

Add Rows to Data Frame

The syntax to add a row to data frame is:

```
rbind(myFrame, newFrame)
```

rbind(myFrame, newFrame) can combine two data frames, which means adding some new rows to a data frame.

In order to add some new rows, you must create a new data frame first.

Example 8.2

Create a data frame, and then create a new data frame.

```
myFrame <- data.frame(

id = c(1:5),

name = c("Andy","Rose","Macy","Dany","Judy"),

score = c(85,99,95,92,96),

year = c("2009", "2002", "2008", "2006", "2007"),

stringsAsFactors = FALSE

)
# Create a new data frame "newFrame".

newFrame <- data.frame(

id = c(6,7),      # column1

name = c("Jony","Tomy"),     # column2

score = c(88,90),      # column3

year = c("2003", "2000"),     # column4
```

```
stringsAsFactors = FALSE

)

# add a row named "newFrame" to the data frame

addRows <- rbind(myFrame, newFrame)

print(addRows)
```

Output:

```
  id name score year
1  1 Andy    85 2009
2  2 Rose    99 2002
3  3 Macy    95 2008
4  4 Dany    92 2006
5  5 Judy    96 2007
6  6 Jony    88 2003
7  7 Tomy    90 2000
```

Explanation:

"rbind(myFrame, newFrame)" combines two data frames, which means adding some rows to the original data frame.

The id 6 and id 7 are new rows.

Combine Vectors

The syntax to combine vectors is:

```
cbine(vector1, vector2, vector3...)
```

"cbine(vector1, vector2, vector3...)" can combine vectors and create a data frame.

Example 8.3

```
# create three vectors
id <- c("001","002","003","004")
name <- c("Anna","Judy","Tony","Nacy")
age <- c(18,16,20,19)
# combine above three vectors into one data frame.
dataFrame <- cbind(id,name,age)
# print the data frame.
print(dataFrame)
```

Output:

```
        id    name    age
[1,] "001" "Anna" "18"
[2,] "002" "Judy" "16"
[3,] "003" "Tony" "20"
[4,] "004" "Nacy" "19"
```

Explanation:

"cbind(id,name,age)" combines three vectors "id, name, age", then create a new data frame.

Combines Data Frames

The syntax to combine two data frames is:

rbine(dataFrame1, dataFrame2)

rbine( ) can combine two data frames.

Example 8.4

```
# create the first data frame "dataFrame1"
id <- c("001","002","003","004")
name <- c("Anna","Judy","Tony","Nacy")
age <- c(18,16,20,19)
# combine above three vectors into one data frame.
dataFrame1 <- cbind(id,name,age)     # dataFrame1
print(dataFrame1)
```

Output: (dataFrame1)

```
        id    name    age
[1,] "001"  "Anna"  "18"
[2,] "002"  "Judy"  "16"
[3,] "003"  "Tony"  "20"
[4,] "004"  "Nacy"  "19"
```

Example 8.5

```
# create the second data frame "dataFrame2".

id <- c("005","006")

name <- c("Otta","Mara")

age <- c(13,15)

# combine above three vectors into one data frame.

dataFrame2 <- cbind(id,name,age)    # dataFrame2

print(dataFrame2)
```

Output: (dataFrame2)

```
       id    name    age
[1,] "005" "Otta" "13"
[2,] "006" "Mara" "15"
```

Example 8.6

```
# combine dataFrame1 and dataFrame2

dataFrame <- rbind(dataFrame1, dataFrame2)

print(dataFrame)
```

Output:

```
      id   name   age
[1,] "001" "Anna" "18"

[2,] "002" "Judy" "16"

[3,] "003" "Tony" "20"

[4,] "004" "Nacy" "19"

[5,] "005" "Otta" "13"

[6,] "006" "Mara" "15"
```

Explanation:

rbind(dataFrame1, dataFrame2) combines two data frames.

R Packages

The R language packages contain a collection of R functions, encoding and sample data. Different packages include different functions. Additional packages can be added as needed when certain functionality is required.

By default, the R language installs only one set of packages during installation. The R language package is installed in a directory named "library".

When we use the R editor, only the default packages are used for programming and operations. Other packages must be explicitly loaded to be used.

Check Directory of R Libraries

The syntax to check the path of the R package libraries is:

```
.libPaths()
```

".libPaths ()" can check the path of the R package libraries.

Example 8.7

```
.libPaths()
```

Output:

[1] "C:/Program Files/R/R-3.5.1/library"

Explanation:

The path of all R package libraries locates in the "C:/Program Files/R/R-3.5.1/library"

Note: the library path may be different with your PC's local directory.

View Installed Packages

The syntax to check the installed packages is:

```
library( )
```

"library()" can check the installed R packages.

Example 8.8

```
library()
```

Output:

Packages in library 'C:/Program Files/R/R-3.5.1/library':

base	The R Base Package
boot	Bootstrap Functions (Originally by Angelo Canty for S)
class	Functions for Classification
cluster	"Finding Groups in Data": Cluster Analysis Extended Rousseeuw et al.
codetools	Code Analysis Tools for R
compiler	The R Compiler Package
datasets	The R Datasets Package
foreign	Read Data Stored by 'Minitab', 'S', 'SAS', 'SPSS', 'Stata', 'Systat', 'Weka', 'dBase', ...
graphics	The R Graphics Package
grDevices	The R Graphics Devices and Support for Colours and Fonts
grid	The Grid Graphics Package
KernSmooth	Functions for Kernel Smoothing Supporting Wand & Jones (1995)
lattice	Trellis Graphics for R
MASS	Support Functions and Datasets for Venables and Ripley's MASS
Matrix	Sparse and Dense Matrix Classes and Methods
methods	Formal Methods and Classes

mgcv Estimation	Mixed GAM Computation Vehicle with Automatic Smoothness
nlme	Linear and Nonlinear Mixed Effects Models
nnet Models	Feed-Forward Neural Networks and Multinomial Log-Linear
parallel	Support for Parallel computation in R
rpart	Recursive Partitioning and Regression Trees
spatial	Functions for Kriging and Point Pattern Analysis
splines	Regression Spline Functions and Classes
stats	The R Stats Package
stats4	Statistical Functions using S4 Classes
survival	Survival Analysis
tcltk	Tcl/Tk Interface
tools	Tools for Package Development
translations	The R Translations Package
utils	The R Utils Package

Explanation:

"library()"checks the installed R packages.

Note: the installed packages may be different with your PC's locally installed packages.

View the Using Packages

The syntax to check what packages are being used is:

```
search( )
```

"search ()" can check the current R packages being used.

Example 8.9

```
search()
```

Output:

[1] ".GlobalEnv"   "package:stats"   "package:graphics"
"package:grDevices" "package:utils"   "package:datasets"
"package:methods"

[8] "Autoloads"   "package:base"

Explanation:

"search ()" can check the current R packages being used.

Note: the current using packages may be different with your PC's using packages.

Install New Packages

The syntax to install new packages is:

install.packages("Package Name")

"install.packages" can install new software packages that have certain specified functionality.

Example 8.10

install.packages("XML")

Output:

Warning in install.packages("XML") :

 'lib = "C:/Program Files/R/R-3.5.1/library"' is not writable

--- Please select a CRAN mirror for use in this session ---

trying URL

'https://mirrors.sorengard.com/cran/bin/windows/contrib/3.5/XML_3.98-

1.16.zip'

Content type 'application/zip' length 4602444 bytes (4.4 MB)

downloaded 4.4 MB

package 'XML' successfully unpacked and MD5 sums checked

......

Explanation:

The above message means that "XML" package has been installed.

Load the Package

Before using a package, you must load it into the current R programming environment

```
library("package Name")
```

library( ) can load the specified package to the library.

Example 8.11

```
library("XML")    # load the package
search( )    # check the loaded package
```

Output:

[1] ".GlobalEnv"   **"package:XML"**

[3] "package:stats"   "package:graphics"

[5] "package:grDevices" "package:utils"

[7] "package:datasets" "package:methods"

[9] "Autoloads"   "package:base"

Explanation:

library("XML") loads the XML package to the library.

Search( ) shows all packages that have been loaded.

We can see the "package:XML" that has been loaded now.

Summary

"myFrame $ newColumn" can add columns into a data frame.

rbind(myFrame, newFrame) can combine two data frames, which means adding some new rows into a data frame.

"cbine(vector1, vector2, vector3...)" can combine vectors and create a data frame.

rbine( ) can combine two data frames.

".libPaths ()" can check the path of the R package libraries.

"library()" can check the installed R packages.

"search ()" can check the current using R packages.

"install.packages" can install new software packages that have certain specified functionality.

library( ) can load the specified package to the library.

Appendix

Q & A

Questions

Please choose the correct answer.

1.

myText <- "Hello, World!"

fill in (myText)　　# output the value of "myText"

A. alert

B. echo

C. output

D. print

2.

The comment symbol of R language is **fill in**

A. //

B. /*　*/

C. #

D. (　)

3.

Which following is **not** an assignment operator of R?

A. =

B. ==

C. ->>

D. ->

4.

```
myfunction <- fill in (x, y){   # define a function

num <- x+y

print(num)

}
```

A. function

B. funct

C. method

D. nothing

5.

```
# create a multiple element vector

print( fill in ("apple", "banana", "cherry"))
```

A. a.

B. b

C. c

D. d

6.

matrix(data, nrow, ncol, byrow, fill in)

"data" is the matrix elements.

"nrow" is the number of rows.

"ncol" is the number of columns.

" **fill in** " is the names of the rows and columns.

A. name

B. dimnames

C. matrix

D. dinnames

7.

factor(data, levels, labels, ...)

factor() can create a factor object.

"data" is a data vector, such as 1:10, c("a", "b", "c").

"levels" is a level vector, whose value is **fill in**.

"labels" is a label vector, just like naming a factor.

A. repeated

B. recurring

C. repetitive

D. unique

8.

"myFrame $ newColumn" can add columns to a **fill in**.

A. array.

B. matrix

C. factor

D. data frame

9.

"**fill in**(variable)" can check the data type of a variable.

A. class

B. check

C. view

D. verify

10.

185

Variable Name	Validity
myVariable	valid
myVariable%	invalid
my_Variable	valid
_myVariable	invalid
myVariable28	valid
26myVariable	invalid
.myVariable	valid
.123	**fill in**

A. valid

B. invalid

C. unlimited

D. undefined

11.

```
> r1<- c(10,13,19)
> r2<- c(3,4,5)
> print(r1 fill in r2)    # get the remainder
```

A. %

B. %%

C. %%%

D. %/%

12.

```
myfunction <- function(x, y){

num <- x+y

fill in(num)   # return the result to the caller

}
```

A. print

B. get

C. cat

D. return

13.

seq(v1, v2, by = step) can create a **fill in** from v1 to v2, by = step specifies the distance among each element.

A. array

B. matrix

C. vector

D. factor

14.

print(**fill in**)

accesses myMatrix element at row 2 and column 3.

A. myMatrix(2,3)

B. myMatrix{2,3}

C. myMatrix<2,3>

D. myMatrix[2,3]

15.

> **fill in** <- c("A","C","B","B", "C","A")

> myfactor = **factor**(data, labels=c("apple", "banana", "cherry"))

> print(myfactor)

A. myVector

B. data

C. vector

D. myArray

16.

fill in(myFrame, newFrame) can combine two data frames, which means adding some new rows to a data frame.

A. rbind

B. rebind

C. combine

D. recombine

17.

Create a vector.

colors <- **fill in**("blue","pink","gray")

print(colors)

A. a

B. b

C. c

D. d

18.

> r1<- c(10,13,19)

> r2<- c(3,4,5)

> print(r1 **fill in** r2)   # get the modulus

A. %

B. %%

C. %%%

D. %/%

19.

```
> v <- fill in
> print(v)
# The output will be   [1] 1 2 3 4 5 6 7 8
```

A. [1,8]

B. 1:8

C. 1 & 8

D. 1 to 8

20.

```
print(fill in(81))   # get the square root
```

A. square

B. sqr

C. squt

D. sqrt

21.

```
> v <- c("apple", "banana", "cherry", "Durian")
> print( v[fill in] )   # remove the 2rd element by index
```

A. remove 2

B. delete 2

C. c(-2)

D. c(2)

22.

dimnames = **fill in**(rownames, colnames)

fill in(rownames, colnames) defines the names for each row and column.

A. list

B. name

C. c

D. function

23.

What is the output of the following code?

> data <- c("A","C","B","B", "C","A")

> myfactor=**factor**(data)

> print(myfactor)

Output:

[1] A C B B C A

Levels: **fill in**

A. A

B. AB

C. ABC

D. ABCBCA

24.

"**fill in**(vector1, vector2, vector3...)" can combine vectors and create a data frame.

A. rbine

B. cbine

C. combine

D. recombine

25.

The **fill in** function can output the value of a variable to the screen as well as to a file, and can print the output continuously.

A. ant( )

B. bear( )

C. cat( )

D. dog( )

26.

```
var <- c("Very Good!")
num <- 0
repeat {
  print(var)
  num <- num+1
  if(num >= 5) {
    fill in    # stop the loop
  }
}
```

A. stop

B. terminate

C. end

D. break

27.

```
> m <- 200
> n <- 100
> if(m < n) {
+    print("m is less than n")
```

+ } **fill in** {

+   print ("m is greater than n")

+ }

A. else

B. otherwise

C. or

D. if not

28.

> a="C#"

> b="in"

> c="8"

> d="Hours"

> **fill in** (a, b, c, d)

[1] "C# in 8 Hours"

A. connect

B. join

C. concat

D. paste

29.

```
> myList <- list(2:6)   # create a list

> myVector <- fill in (myList)   # convert list to a vector

> print(myVector)
```

A. convert

B. unlist

C. update

D. tovector

30.

```
vector1 <- c(1,2,3)

vector2 <- c(4,5,6,7,8,9)

myArray <- array(c(vector1,vector2),dim = c(3,3,1))

# sort the array elements

result3 <- fill in (myArray, c(3), sort)

print(result3)
```

A. sort

B. sequence

C. apply

D. arrange

31.

The **fill in** function can view the structure of the data frames.

A. str( )

B. structure( )

C. struct( )

D. frame( )

32.

"**fill in**" function can check the current using R packages.

A. .libPaths()

B. library()

C. package()

D. search()

Answers

01	D	17	C
02	C	18	D
03	B	19	B
04	A	20	D
05	C	21	C
06	B	22	A
07	D	23	C
08	D	24	B
09	A	25	C
10	B	26	D
11	B	27	A
12	D	28	D
13	C	29	B
14	D	30	C
15	B	31	A
16	A	32	D

Recommended Books by Ray Yao

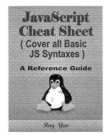

(Each Cheat Sheet contains more than 300 examples, more than 300 outputs, and more than 300 explanations.)

Paperback Books by Ray Yao

C# Cheat Sheet

C++ Cheat Sheet

Java Cheat Sheet

JavaScript Cheat Sheet

Php MySql Cheat Sheet

Python Cheat Sheet

Html Css Cheat Sheet

Linux Command Line

C# 100 Q & A

C++ 100 Q & A

Java 100 Q & A

JavaScript 100 Q & A

Php MySql 100 Q & A

Python 100 Q & A

Html Css 100 Q & A

Linux 100 Q & A

C# Examples

C++ Examples

Java Examples

JavaScript Examples

Php MySql Examples

Python Examples

Html Css Examples

Shell Scriptng Examples

Advanced C++ in 8 hours

Advanced Java in 8 hours

AngularJs in 8 hours

C# programming

C++ programming

Dart in 8 hours

Django in 8 hours

Erlang in 8 hours

Git Github in 8 hours

Golang in 8 hours

Google Sheets in 8 hours

Haskell in 8 hours

Html Css programming

Java programming

JavaScript programming

JQuery programming
Kotlin in 8 hours
Lua in 8 hours
Matlab in 8 hours
Matplotlib in 8 hours
MySql database
Node.Js in 8 hours
NumPy in 8 hours
Pandas in 8 hours
Perl in 8 hours
Php MySql programming
PowerShell in 8 hours
Python programming
R programming
React.Js in 8 hours
Ruby programming
Rust in 8 hours
Scala in 8 hours
Shell Scripting in 8 hours
Swift in 8 hours
TypeScript in 8 hours
Visual Basic programming
Vue.Js in 8 hours
Xml Json in 8 hours